T0157792

God's Grace

"*faith*"cfd

iUniverse, Inc.
Bloomington

God's Grace

iUniverse books may be ordered through booksellers or by contacting:

iUniverse
1663 Liberty Drive
Bloomington, IN 47403
www.iuniverse.com
1-800-Authors (1-800-288-4677)

ISBN: 978-1-4620-0544-4 (pbk)
ISBN: 978-1-4620-0545-1 (ebk)

Printed in the United States of America

iUniverse rev. date: 3/29/11

Dedicated To

JESUS

---

†

Clara Ann Moran

Edward Davidson

Table of Contents

For The Lady

We've come a long and tiresome way
Nothing short of a miracle you might say
Years of hurt and aggravation
Still your love and motivation
Makes me love you more you see
With your help I've grown to be
Level headed and respected
Probably more than you expected
Always there though far away
Closer than ever we have stayed
I know at times I made it rough
You Dear Lady were always so tough
When know one here could get through
I knew I could call and talk to you
You'd listen to me for ever so long
And you learned to read me when something was wrong
You can tell before I can say
Lady I'm glad that it's that way
Sometime I'm not sure I should impose
But I love you a lot and I suppose
That if you didn't love me you wouldn't ask
And try to break through my I'm "ok" mask
Your always there when I call
To help me up when I fall
Numerous years you've been my friend
And I know now it will never end
You've been so patient kind and true
No matter what I tried to do

cont.

For The Lady (cont.)
You know the hurts that I still feel
And when their gnawing you help me deal
I call you Mom I love you so
Lady I just want you to know
I thank you for the love you've shown
Your loves lasted longer than any I've known
When I was young I was very bad
My hostility toward you would make you mad
You didn't back up you didn't walk away
Numerous years your love has stayed
When they hurt me as they often do
I know I can always run to you
"No" comes easier to me these days
It's taken some work to change my ways
You've been with me through bad and good
Giving me love my parents never could
I thank God for you Lady and pray everyday
I'll never hurt you again in anyway
I love you so deeply I really do
But this is something you already knew
You are so special and so strong
I'm thankful this love has lasted so long
I can't say enough how much I care
It's so important to me to know your there
I hope this brings a smile to you
To know I love you as I do
So in closing I say to you
I Love you Dear Lady I really do...
                    "faith"cfd

MOM

She's my best friend in good and bad this Lady I call Mom
She's always there no matter what to help the storms to calm
She reads me like an open book but I've torn the pages out
Doesn't matter she still knows, that's what Mom is all about
I love this Lady I call Mom she's special and she's kind
She understands, knows the words my way she helps me find
I'm glad the Lord has blessed me for she is good to me
I love this Lady very much and that's how it ought to be
We're far apart yet closer as the years go slipping by
I'll love this Lady I call Mom until the day I die
Without her love and guidance I can't imagine where I'd be
Because Mom's the rock I lean on she means a lot to me
Thank you Lord for giving me this precious Mothers love
Keep her safe, healthy Lord with your light from up above
And if she ever stumbles or needs my help at all
Please Dear God let her know I'm as close as just a call
I'll be there for her always until she's gone from me
Dear Jesus please let a long time pass before that day I see
Because she's such a caring Lady so confident and strong
And like you Lord she loves me even when I wrong
Lord I cannot thank you enough for giving her to me
I pray when life on earth is done she and I with you will be
Bless each Mother Dear Lord for there love and caring
And tune a child's heart into the love there Moms sharing
For a loving Mom is someone it's hard to live without
This Lady whom I call Mom is precious without a doubt
I love You Mom

"faith" cfd

Mom Is The Best Ever

Mom's love is the most precious love that I know today
Only Mom, she's the one that makes me feel this way
Motivation,that gentle push she's always given me

I haven't always felt this way, but now I plainly see
She's always been so tough, so strong and bold yet true

That's why that I am older, I do for her all that I can do
Having such a special friend, a confidant and guide,
Ever caring and so loving, she's always by my side

Because I think she's special, she's beautiful to me.
Everlasting is my love for her, like her I want to be.
Standing in the shadows, I'll see her with her crown,
The Lady that I love so much won't always be around.

Everyday growing older, and stronger grows our love,
Very thankful Lord am I for your light from up above
Ever grateful for the presence of the love from Mother!
Remembering to thank you Lord, for there will never be
another! ! !

"faith"cfd

Long Time Bond

I'm setting in the first lights
        of and early morning dawn
Where in the distance I can see
        where all the clouds have gone
Your on my mind so strong
        and clear as though your by my side
The bond we share is special
        and in you I can confide
When we met I was a child
        in body in soul and mind
For I loved you so very fast
        like no one else I'll ever find
My love for you has only grown
        much deeper as the years went by
For stronger then ever it is now
        I love you dearly I can't lie
I get such a warming feeling
        whenever your around
A feeling of contentment
        with no one else I've ever found
But you know it really scares me
        for when I love so deep
I seem to suffocate the one
        I try so hard to keep
But with you it's never been
        an effort so easy it has come
To spite our ups and downs
        and we know there has been some
Never have I ever thought
        of not loving you anymore
        (cont.)

Long Time Bond (cont.)
For there's a long time strong time bond
                I've never had before
I know you'll always love me
                in spite of things I do
As I will always love you
                I cherish this love too
I know we've grown over the years
                in a lot of different ways
But one thing has stayed the same
                I've loved you all those days
If the truth be really known
                of which I've never told
It's a good thing we do live apart
                for trouble would unfold
Because I'd want you close to me
                and wear out my welcome fast
And kill the love that's grown so strong
                and I really want to last
You've always had a tender touch
                and could always ease my mind
I could look forever more
                and not another like this I'd find
For it's just special strong
                and clear there's never been a doubt
That I love you and you love me
                that's what it's all about
I just wanted you to know
                just how dear you are to me
I love you more than words can say
                that's how it will always be
                                "faith" cfd

God Talks

God talks to you when your listening
When you hear him your eyes are glistening
He's made up his mind, with Jesus you'll find
The peace that you need for your troubled mind
God talks to you there is no doubt
For Jesus the Christ is your only out
All things can be done through Jesus the King
With Jesus you can and will do anything
Just trust Jesus in your heart
And surely he will do his part
To ease your mind and bring you peace
So all the heartache then will cease
Just go to Jesus in your prayer
For Christ the King is everywhere
                    "faith" cfd

Forever

Help me dear Jesus so when you descend
The rest of forever with you I will spend
Help me to see that all you adore
And help me to reach your open door
Be with me and help me this life to endure
And be with me Jesus for your love is sure
I'm sure Dear Jesus that you are my friend
And will be with me always right up to the end
You'll speak to me always if I can just hear
As you speak to me you could draw a sweet tear
For listening to you goes right to my heart
I know with you Jesus that we'll never part
                              "faith"cfd

Talk to Me

Hello Jesus my dearest friend
I've come to speak with you again
I'm here to pray down on my knees
And ask you Jesus to speak to me please
Tell me you love me in your gentle way
And help me to listen to what you might say
Help me understand and help me to see
Just what it is your asking of me
Take me Jesus take over my life
Teach me my Master there will be strife
That times won't be easy all of the way
And help me dear Jesus away I'll not stray
Dear Jesus please take me into your loving care
So in death that great mansion with you I will share

"faith"cfd

Jesus Is

Jesus is my savior true
He tells me what I should do
He walks beside me everyday
And at night he hears me pray
I pray for peace and joy and love
I pray someday I see the dove
The mansion is in the heavens high
The glorious place up in the sky
A place where God and Jesus stay
And send the holy spirit my way
To keep me strong and dry my eyes
My savior Jesus in the sky

"faith"cfd

Jesus the Master
Our Master is so tried and true
He knows just what he wants us to do
Be patient and listen be quiet and still
The Master the Lord will tell us his will
He'll help us achieve everything that he asks
And help us to do all of our tasks
Just listen and hear what the Master will say
All tasks he will help us in his special way
Help us he'll help us he will make us strong
And forgive all the things that we might do wrong
For Jesus the Master our Savior and friend
Will be right be side me till the very end
                              "faith"cfd

His People
For God so loved the world it seemed
He sent Jesus to realize all of our dreams
Jesus the Master is our dearest friend
He'll be with us always and help us to bend
Bend over backwards to help one another
Our mother our father our sister our brother
To help every stranger not just our kin
Not just family and not just our friend
Every one in the world it seems
Will do Jesus work for that is his scheme
To love on another to be faithful and kind
For a friend in Jesus is the best we will find
A friend to all people our Master and Lord
Even when we are sad or when we are bored
He'll help us to see what he wants us to do
For Jesus the Master does love me and you
                              "faith"cfd

"Patience"

Be patient my child just be still and listen
For if you do this you'll see your eyes glisten
You'll smile your mind will come to a peace
All your troubles will come to a cease
The trouble you feel may not go away
Patience be still there will be a better day
For God will make all the bad go away
Just be strong and faithful please stay
For with Jesus there'll be a new day
And Jesus will be with you all of your way
And love Dear Jesus with all that you can
For he is the Master the Great Son of Man
"faith"cfd

"Did You?"

Twilight is a perfect time of day
To contemplate the ones who've passed your way
Did you speak of God did you spread the news good
Of Jesus our Lord like he tells we should
Did you hold out your hand to someone in need
And take the time to plant a good seed
Did you smile at a stranger and say "How are you"
Or did you walk on and go do what you do
Did you see someone struggling and lend them a hand
For there is such suffering in this our great land
Say Jesus can help you just try to believe
For Heaven is greater than you can perceive
Jesus our Savior our Lord and our King
With Jesus the Christ you can do anything
"faith"cfd

I Love You So

I love you Son I love you dearly
I just wish you learn to see life more clearly
To accept life's responsibilities
And see what God wants you to see
To be a strong man to be gentle and kind
All of this and more with Jesus you'll find
Find a place be quiet and read
And on the Holy Ghost please feed
Learn what God wants from you
Then all will become clear and you'll know what to do
Find solitude find peace find love in the Lord
Just read your bible when you become bored
It's written down it's there Son it's there
And know that are God he does really care
He cares for us always wherever we are
He sent baby Jesus under that shining star
He loves you I know it for I love him too
Just take my advice he wants to love you
Just open your heart and let him in son
And let him love you as we have done
"faith"cfd

For Steven

Gods Children
Be faithful and true to the Holy Father
Take the time to go on and bother
And take the time to help others
For we are all sisters and brothers
One to another one and all
God doesn't want anyone to fall
He wants all his children to have pleasant peace
To stop the trails and all tears to cease
He will come back that's what Jesus said
And all Gods children will be happy and fed
Children of God heed him and pray
For Jesus our king will see in heaven one day
                              "faith"cfd

                    "Lord"
You are my savior my Lord and my King
For you dear Jesus I'd do anything
I'd climb a steep mountain I'd swim a great sea
Because all that I am is what you've made me
To be strong and happy and go that mile
You make it much easier to do with a smile
Take me and make me all that you can
For Jesus I Love you with all that I am
Heartfelt is my Love for you my great Master
I just wish I would learn just a little bit faster
I'm slow but I try to be patient as I can
For someday I'll see you dear Lord Son of Man
                              "faith"cfd

"Faithful"
Maybe someday I'll write a book
So in my soul you all can look
The time seems bad in growing older
But steadfast Love has made me a soldier
Of love and peace and kindness too
All the things that I should do
I'll be faithful to God because I feel chosen
To be his child even when my eyes are closing
And God's the one to bring me peace
With him alone my troubles will cease
He makes me smile and he makes me sure
There is nothing on earth I can't endure
My God my friend I love you so
But this my Lord you already know
                              "faith"cfd

Take Time to Pray
Take time to pray for Jesus hears
If you'll let him he'll dry your tears
He'll lift you up and hold you tight
And get you softly through day and night
Take time to pray to our Holy Father
And Satan's ways you will not bother
He'll lead you guide you and make you whole
And God will have your eternal soul
Take time to pray for others always
For prayer can help in so many ways
Take the time to pray be faithful and true
Let God be there to comfort you
He's there to help he knows your need
Just be still and let him plant his seed
Help it grow and you will see
How much God Loves you and me
                              "faith"cfd

"Grace"
Amazing Grace is Gods alone
All he wants is to take us home
To Love and care and ease our mind
No other Grace you'll ever find
For God is good and loves us all
And never wants to see us fall
Hold up your hands and and sing his praise
And have peace of mind for all your days
Be calm be strong for Gods sweet love
Comes to us from up above
He's there be true be kind and fair
For in Heaven someday you'll see him there
"faith"cfd

"My God"
So kind so strong so utterly fair
Please God I want to come up there
My friend my strength my precious God
Take me to Heaven were my feet can trod
The paradise it's beauty sweet
Let me sit at your precious feet
Help me be strong and fair and just
And learn the things you say I must
Be by my side through good and bad
And lift me up when I am sad
Help me be faithful strong and true
And do all the things you ask me to do
And take me home when the time is right
My God my friend I'll put up no fight
I'll come with a smile upon my face
To see my God and all of his Grace
"faith"cfd

You and Me

Take heed God has an open hand
He rules the earth and all it's land
God wants to mold us set us free
He only wants whats best for thee
Take heed for God is watching you
In every single thing you do
He sent his Son to die for us
To feel Gods Love is just a must
Jesus is our savior so dear
And knowing that should bring a tear
A tear of joy will see us through
All the trails in life that we must do
He is our rock our Lord and our friend
Jesus will be with us to the very end
He'll walk with us and hold us tight
And watch over us as we sleep at night
His loving face someday we will behold
For that is what the bible has told
Be strong lift up your head and smile
The trails will only last awhile
Be kind help out as you can see
God Loves all of us that's you and that's me
                    "faith"cfd

The Kingdom

Dear Jesus let me see your bright light
And know that I'm down here and still in your sight
Let me know your up yonder
And help me to grow in your Love even fonder
I'll take up my cross and do as you ask
And someday with humbleness in Heaven I'll bask
I'll sit at your feet and glow like a star
To know that you are who you say that you are
To be in Heaven so quiet and sweet
And know that my Lord my Jesus I'll meet
My heart will glow brightly as never before
And to let you know Jesus that you I adore
Adore your sweet smile your strength and your Love
And to know that I made it to the kingdom above
                                    "faith" cfd

Your Way

Jesus Jesus my precious friend
Help keep me strong until the end
Keep me safe from all the worlds harms
Until I can feel your sweet sweet arms
Guide me lead me where I should go
And teach me Master what I must know
Tell me the things that I must do
So when I die I will see you
Caress me with your loving way
So someday I can hear you say
Well done my child you've served me well
Because at my feet your burdens fell
You trusted me to help you through
All the things I asked of you
Well done Well Done my child I say
For you have surely found your way
                                    "faith" cfd

Help Me

You have a puppy? let it run
That's the way God wants it done
Be free from care and just believe
God will bring more than you perceive
Take heart be proud for God's the one
That gave to us his only Son
To care for us and help us through
All the things he wants us to do
He'll love and hold us in his hand
Until the day we leave this land
He'll guide us lead us in his way
Lord help us is all we need to say

"faith" cfd

Watching

Jesus Jesus is the King
He is the King of everything
Your house your child your car as well
Jesus knows and he can tell
We believers are struggling bad
But Jesus wants us to be glad
He's there we just can't see him now
But to care for us is his vow
To take us in his loving arms
And cradle us in his heavenly charms
One day the King will take us home
And we'll see our God upon his thrown
With Jesus there by Gods side
Smiling gently with such pride
And welcoming his children home
As he watched us from his thrown
God is with us Jesus too
So do the way that you should do
Be kind and loving cool and meek
For Jesus reigns over the weak
He watches us all through the day
Even while we sleep he will stay
He's always there he's there it's true
He's always there he's watching you
He's watching and he knows it all
He doesn't want one child to fall
Believe do good kneel down and pray
For God won't have it any other way
Be faithful and you will see
In Heaven with Jesus you will be
                    "faith" cfd

Only Son

See the mountains standing tall
With mounds of snow that cover all
And little ones are down below
Laughing playing in the snow
God has his hand on everyone
Mother daughter father son
Although sometime we're unaware
Jesus the Son is always there
To hold our hands and make us strong
With so many things going wrong
Take heed be brave keep holding on
Time will pass and they'll all be gone
A glorious Mansion will be our prize
If only we can visualize
God loves us each and everyone
For he sent Jesus his only Son
                    "faith"cfd

Troubled Mind

We're in a time of great tribulation
People fighting and dieing from Nation to Nation
God sees the things that are going on
But on that day Gabriel will blow his horn
And come for us that do believe
In Jesus only God conceived
Jesus the Master and the King
Will come and lighten everything
He'll shine so bright he'll hurt your eyes
And people will drop to there knees and cry
Sweet Jesus come and take me home please
And set my troubled mind at ease
                    "faith"cfd

"Blessings"
Thank you for your blessing of Jesus Chris our King
Thank you for your blessing Lord thank you for everything
Thank you for your blessing our family our home our car as well
Thank you for your blessing for some they cannot tell
Thank you for your blessing let us be prepared to share
Thank you for your blessing help us always care
Thank you for your blessing let all the people show
Thank you for your blessing dear Lord we love you so
Thank you for your blessing our Lord our God our friend
Thank you for your blessing we'll love you till the end
"faith"cfd

"People Go"
Religious people need to know
The extra mile they must go
To bring the ones of sin to God
So they can walk on Heavens sod
To feel the need of Jesus love
And know he loves us from above
To know he's there through thick and thin
And know the pleasure of forgiven sin
Hold hands with the King and all his Glory
And tell all the sinners all about his story
Tell them of Christ and his loving arms
Of all his Glory and all his charms
How patient and strong kind and true
People go and do what God has asked of you
Pray for the sinners as you fall to your knees
Pray that the devil from everyone flees
Fall to your knees and ask God to show
All of the things that you need to know
People go and be humble
For all sinners will stumble
Go and help them up
So with God they can sup
Go with God our Mighty King
For with God we can do anything
"faith"cfd

He Protects Us

Do you have the armor of God
Which helps us through this world that we trod
Having your loins girded with truth all around
And the breastplate of righteousness securely bound
And your feet shod with the gospel of peace
Do you have the shield of faith for the darts to cease
And put the helmet of Salvation on your head
Because this is what our Lord has said
Fight the Devil, don't let him win
For you don't want to live a life of sin
Do this because God knows what is right
And you will gain favor in Gods sight
Be careful Satan is sneaky and shrewd
Use Gods great word as your food
Read the word and God will help you
Everyday in whatever you might do
Be faithful in the word and live
And all Gods promises to you he will give
                              "faith"cfd

Up and Down

I think of Jesus when I am down
For he has the power to put my feet on the ground
I smile when I'm lonely, I smile when I'm sad
And Jesus will help me get rid of the bad
Pray Jesus please help me I'm fading away
Dear Jesus please help me get through this bad day
Comfort and hold me in your loving care
Tell me my burdens with you I should share
Take me Lord show me the things I should know
May all of my sadness away it should go
When I am down and just can't go on
Remind me Dear Jesus that I am reborn
Remind me that sickness has no direction
You know when I feel that there is no connection
Remind me in Heaven all sickness is cured
And make my heart happy and so gently stirred
Remind me in Heaven I'll be with you Master
And maybe the pain will go away faster
And show me the sadness will soon fade away
Just faithful and true to you Jesus I'll stay

"faith" cfd

Those

Alas the time is growing near
When God will take away the fear
All will be gone it will all pass away
For those with Jesus Christ have stayed
Those who tried those who did succeed
Those who helped the people in need
Those with a prayer for someone else
Not just a prayer about them self
Those who put out all that they had
And all the times those made someone glad
Those of power and those of wealth
Those who gave away them self
Those that felt Gods pulling need
Those that planted all there seed
And nurtured the seed they sow
Without boasting loudly for all to know
Quietly somberly humbly those pray
The seed would grow and be ready that day
The day the Lord comes for his own
The day that Jesus carries us home
Those who belong to Jesus you know
To Heaven sweet Heaven with Jesus we'll go
For that's the main reason that we do believe
Jesus the Son of Man To awesome to perceive
For some will go and some will stay
Where will you be on Jesus day

"faith" cfd

He Helps Me
When I feel bad my spirits down
I don't want people all around
Because pain and people just don't mix
This is a problem only God can fix
I try to take it all in stride
But I have this thing and it's called pride
I don't want people seeing I'm blue
But sometimes that's so hard to do
I know the Lord has a place for me
If only I'll take the time to see
There's a reason for all this trial
I'll know in time it just takes awhile
He'll lift me up and hold me tight
With Jesus help I know I'll stand
He'll carry me walk with me he's always there
Precious Jesus my Lord thanks for your care
"faith"cfd

"Sinners"

All of the people that God calls his own
Will be by his side when he carries us home
For in the Bible It says people rejoice
And know that everyone does have a choice
To be close to God and Jesus his Son
Or be with the devil when Jesus shall come
Please sinners recognize the strife
What being with Satan will bring to your life
Jesus the Christ is the only way
For when he comes oh what a great day
A day for believers all lifted up high
Below the sinners that kneel down and cry
For they didn't believe or thought there was time
For your salvation is gone and it's such a crime
For it will be to late you can't get in
Because you chose to go with your sin
We pray that all sinners will come and find
That salvation is something you need in your mind
Come with us dear sinners come with us we pray
So you can come also on that glorious day
And Jesus will take you to Heaven so sweet
The only place our God can you meet
Come with us dear sinners he will let you in
Just believe in Jesus for he is your friend
Your friend your King the precious Lord
Please live with Jesus and not by the sword
Come with us dear sinners we ask as a friend
Sinners come with us when earth comes to an end
For the end could come real soon
Even during the fullest moon
Come with us we pray that's all we can do
All of the rest is left up to you

"faith"cfd

Glory to See

Glory to God for Jesus the King
With Jesus we can do anything
He'll help us he'll lead us he'll hold our hand
We must stick together and form a great band
A band of soldiers that worship the king
For only good our patience will bring
He's here in our midst he's never to far
He's watchful he's patient wherever we are
He'll give us the strength we need to get by
He'll be right beside us whenever we cry
Cry out to the Master he'll be by your side
When the time comes in Heaven we'll abide
Sweet Heaven with God and with Jesus too
All you do is what he's asking of you
Just follow his word and know that someday
The Savior will come and take us away
To Heaven to Heaven what Glory to see
Will be all that is left for you and for me

"faith" cfd

We Can

Take up your cross ,
                and follow me
So Heavens sod,
                one day you'll see
Heavens so beautiful,
                it's just divine
No better place,
                will you ever find
A mansion is promised,
                when I get there
All I think I could do,
                is stand there and stare
All the wonder and Glory,
                that I have been told
In the New Testament,
                and also the Old
Jesus is the Man,
                the Son of God by name
To abide in his loving care,
                I'll never be the same
So trust in Jesus all your life,
                he is the Son of Man
And know that everything we do,
                with Jesus we know we can
                "faith"cfd

See

Let me in says the Lord
Come to me put down your sword
Praise my name be Glory bond
For the love of Jesus trumpets sound
Take up your cross and follow me
A soldier of God then you will be
A mighty soldier that is right
For Jesus now you must fight
Spread the word be humble yet
For persecution you may get
For people are afraid of God
Thin ice is where so many trod
They take the risk of falling through
But believers know what we're to do
We praise the Lord we let him in
We try so hard not to sin
When we sin we go to Jesus
For he alone will forgive us
Listen people near and far
Jesus knows just where you are
He's there he's here he's at your door
Let him in that's what he's here for
To bring you peace of mind each day
To teach you humbly how to pray
For everyone not just yourself
Please don't put Jesus on a shelf
Take him down and praise his name
And you will never be the same
Love the Lord as your very own
Soon he will be here to take you home
Jesus is where your heart should be
People please people our Jesus please see
"faith" cfd

Turmoil

It's awful how the world is now
Fussing fighting all crying fowl
Know one knows how to get along
Know one knows how to sing a song
Just fuss and fight and watch people die
Makes me just want to lay down and cry
For this is not how it should be
At least not the way God wants to see
Stop fussing stop fighting stop fouling around
Stop all this nonsense put your feet on the ground
Be kind to each other for God has said
He counts every hair that is on your head
He's crying he's sobbing up on his thrown
Wondering if they'll be one to bring home
He sees the tragedy he sees the unrest
He sees all the cause it weighs on his chest
Heaven the kingdom it's hard to see
Just love the Lord and peaceful you'll be
Take time to feel love don't fuss and don't fight
For God really loves you and your in his sight
One day he will come to take his own home
How many will be left to sit here and moan
How many will miss the most Glorious day
Cause fussing and fighting has got in the way
Slow down and pray not just when it's bad
But always forever and never be sad
Don't be left behind repent and praise
For God will come to us one of these days
He'll come and take his people home
Please don't be left here alone
Take God as your protector true
For you know that God loves you
                    "faith" cfd

"God"
Tell it sell it God is King
Shout from a high we can do anything
Let people know that God is the one
People must know that God gave his Son
Feed the people sow the seed
God is what the people need
All are not without sin
God is here to take us in
Let him abide deep in your heart
And never ever shall you part
God is love God is kindness
People take away your blindness
Open up your hearts and see
God is all there will ever be
"faith"cfd

Jesus Paid

Be brave be calm says our God
For Heavens great walkways you will trod
Heavens just one step away
I love Jesus you must say
To love the King means you believe
That's what God wants you to conceive
That Jesus gave his life for you
To cleanse your soul and make you new
If you love Jesus then celebrate
Then Heaven will be your fate
And such a fate will be divine
A better friend you'll never find
A Savior who wipes away your sin
All he asks is just let him in
He'll be your bodyguard through life
Let him help you with the strife
He's here he loves you let him in
Jesus the King paid for our sin
He's paid the price the debt is done
Don't let him in and the devil has won
All he asks is to believe in him
Just believe and let him in

"faith"cfd

Ask

Gods the King the Master and more
He always hears what we ask him for
He doesn't always do what we ask him to
But he lets us know what he wants us to do
He'll give us what we need though it may not be
Just what we want but we must always see
That what we want may not be his plan
But believe that God holds us tight in his hand
In time we'll understand what his is to be
Although it may not be what we want to see
But be sure that the Master knows what is best
For he holds us all deeply against his great chest
He hopes as he watches and holds us we'll hold to him to
And hopes we'll understand what for us he will do
For he is the Master the Lord and the King
With God and his Son we can do anything
                                    "faith" cfd

When We're Done

 God I love you I'll pray till the end
That when I go the angels you'll send
To bring me home and the mansion I'll see
That you share with others and you'll share with me
I'll set at your feet and see your great face
And life on earth will take second place
For in Heaven I'll be when the end comes for me
Surrounded by others who prayed this day to see
We'll make it to Glory land sweet as a fountain
And know that no longer will we climb that mountain
For we will be done we'll be happy and free
As we'll be in Heaven where we want to be
Will be in Heaven with God and Jesus our King
And we'll know it was true we could do anything
                                    "faith" cfd

Stay

Dear Jesus my King I do love you
Tell me this day what I should do
To help myself my friends and foe
To get to where we need to go
To hold the power of the King
With him we can do anything
Anything that's what I need
Please help me Jesus to succeed
My knees are bent my hands are together
Help me Lord this storm to weather
It's not just me but others too
We all need to know what we should do
To satisfy your steadfast ways
To be with you in our eternal days
Jesus help me be kind and true
And help me in all that I will do
For the time will soon come I know
That to Heaven with my Lord I'll go
I'll go to Heaven bright and sweet
And lay my burdens at your feet
For then all things will pass away
And with my Lord I'll forever stay

"faith"cfd

Please Listen

Dear Lord I need you now
At your blessed feet I bow
I need your comfort for I'm in pain
If you don't help I'll go insane
Things are hard and times are tough
I need your help with all this stuff
Help me hold on help me stay
Please listen Lord to what I say
Please help me Lord stay in your fold
Help me Lord my hand please hold
Help me stabilize my life
Help me hang on through the strife
Please keep me in your loving sight
And help me to sleep when it is night
Help me to understand this day
And know you'll always show the way
The way of peace and tranquility
Please Dear Lord please speak to me

Please Listen (cont)
Please speak to me and show your love
For someday I hope to see the dove
The Chariot of Jesus true
Who'll bring me there to be with you
When I come home and kneel at your feet
That's when life will become so sweet
No strife no pain it'll all be gone
And nothing else will ever go wrong
Beautiful everything will be
When your precious face I see
I'll kneel and I'll praise you God
On Heavens golden soil I'll trod
Forever and ever and ever more
Please lead me to your open door
And when I come it's open wide
Then I find myself inside
Inside I say I'll make it in
And there I'll find my special friend
God the Father Christ the Son
Now my journey will be done
                    "faith" cfd

Prayer in Need

I pray in the times when I feel so low
And pray in the times when things are so so
But let things go right and God is left out
More low feelings is what this is all about
Be careful to praise God for seeing it through
Or more hard times you'll see for I know I do
Praise the Almighty the Maker of all
With God troubles seem so petty and small
When things look up we forget to pray
When it all goes wrong we come and say
Lord what have I done that was so bad
To punish me with all the troubles I've had
It's not the Lord that causes our grief
But us for not thanking him for the relief
So seek the Lords face everyday bad or good
He'll keep you calm as he promised he would
Be constant with God as he is with you
And better will everything be that you do
                              "faith"cfd

Comfort

As I prayed I bowed my head
And listen to what you have said
I try to hear you I really do
Always when I come to you
But I must learn your always here
To take away all my fear
To comfort me from where you are
Even though you are so far
Far away but still close by
Your here every time I cry
When I look up help me always see
Your hand is on me and will always be
Be beside me and behind me too
So I open my eyes and look for you
You'll be there so gentle and kind
No better friend will I ever find

"faith"cfd

Touch

I'm lost I'm lonely I'm so out of touch
Dear Jesus please help me I need you so much
Wake up this dormant body as only you can
And show me all of when it began
Your birth your life your preaching too
Teach me all that you can for I will do
Anything that you ask as long as I see
The presence of you Lord please show it to me
Take my mind and my body too
Show me what you want me to do
Take hold of my hand and lead me the way
So Jesus my King I'll hear all that you say
Say well done child you've done me proud
And Jesus please let me hear it out loud

"faith"cfd

Unite

Precious Jesus who shed your blood
Open my heart make it a flood
Wash away the awful thought
Fill me full of what you've brought
My minds a blur please fill it in
Show me I'm not suppose to sin
Show me how to walk the street
And speak to everyone I meet
Some don't speak back I wonder why
Maybe they need to sit with you and cry
Cry out I need you please take me in
Take me away from all this sin
Make me mold me a christian to be
All the good I do need to see
Everyone needs to pray a prayer
To help the people everywhere
To unite the people and the king
Would be such a glorious thing
So when the day comes and Jesus arrives
Everyone on earth survives
We'll all go home Lord everyone
To be with you God and Jesus your Son
"faith" cfd

I Know

Jesus you are my best friend
I'll love you until the very end
When the time comes and you appear
For me there won't be any fear
I know my love is steadfast true
I know I'll go home with you
To the open door the open gate
I know my mind is in the right state
A state of mind with Jesus it is
Because I know that I am his
He talks to me he sets me straight
He wants to see me at the gate
To let me in and say well done
For he's of God he is his Son
When it comes the time to go
I'll be with Jesus this I know
                    "faith" cfd

Loving You

Jesus my Savior my Master my King
Thank you for all of the pleasure you bring
Thanks for loving me thanks for your way
Thank you for getting me through everyday
Keep loving me Jesus please don't let me go
For loving you is a privilege I know
A privilege and honer to be your child
No fussing no fighting no going wild
Just passing along the friend that you are
And knowing someday you'll come from afar
Someday Jesus I'll see your face
In Heaven I can't wait to see that place
Because you'll be there upon your thrown
And I'll see your face and know that I'm home
                    "faith" cfd

Answer

Glory to God in the highest I say
Because Jesus the Christ is the only way
The way to salvation the way to peace
And he is the way for all troubles to cease
Ask God to forgive you I know that he will
Ask God in silence just sit and be still
Let his love surround you let him come in
Ask Jesus and he will take all your sin
For God the Father and Jesus his Son
Just want all to know what Jesus has done
He suffered and died he hung on the cross
So none of his people would ever be lost
Yes he is the answer I'll tell you right now
Let him come in and he'll help and how
I want to see Jesus and look on his face
In Heaven I know that you've heard of this place
This place called Heaven so brilliantly bright
Ask God to forgive you when you go to bed at night
He's there he's listening he'll answer your prayer
For then you will know that he's everywhere
He's there to console whenever your down
Just trust in the lord get rid of that frown
Just know that he loves you everyday
And keep him close for he wants it that way
                              "faith"cfd

Rough

Jesus is the one you know
Jesus is the seed you sow
If you believe and you are right
You know your in Gods awesome sight
For know that they are looking down
You can feel them all around
You can feel the peace within
Because Jesus paid for all your sin
He paid the price for us to know
That when we pass to Heaven we'll go
We'll go to Heaven oh how it gleams
But Heaven is so far away it seems
That's alright it'll be soon enough
Until then it may be tough
That's OK for this we know
That in the end to Heaven we'll go
"faith"cfd

Three

Jesus flies like a bird on a wing
He is my Master he is my King
He lifts me up like a cool nights breeze
And makes my mind feel so at ease
Jesus and God gave me the spirit
Open your heart and you can feel it
I feel the power that lives within me
People open your eyes and you will see
That God, Jesus and the Holy Spirit are three
I'm protected by all that's where I want to be
They hold me they take care of my need
And when I'm hungry they always feed
They feed my mind they open my eyes
They wait for me to come to the skies
There always there the one in three
They always hold and comfort me
They watch over me when I'm asleep
The love of God I shall always keep
When I pass on I'm Heaven bond
And I'm really glad I kept them around
"faith"cfd

Believe

The sun is rising in the sky
So far away it's up so high
But higher yet your Heaven gleams
And it's so far away also it seems
Someday I'll be passing on
I know all pain then will be gone
The aches the pains the heartache too
Will all be gone that's what you do
So patient I must be and wait
Until I see that pearly gate
Until the time you call me home
My christian skills I must comb
Keep them neat and wait for you
And do the things you ask me to
Talk to people sow a seed
Try to help the ones in need
Take the people by the hand
And tell them of the promise land
Help them grow and understand
That all Gods children are in his hand
He's here for us he'll take us in
For Jesus died for all our sin
He hung on the cross and died for us
Jesus never made a fuss
They beat him struck him made him bleed
So we would have everything that we need
Maybe not what we thought or even our way
Believe and your dreams will come true someday
Just raise up your hands and pray to the Lord
Take up your cross and lay down your sword
Take up your cross follow Jesus you'll see
When this life is over in Heaven you'll be
"faith" cfd

New Day

It's dawn and the darkness is fading away
Be happy in Jesus he's brought a new day
Be happy be calm be quiet and still
Listen and Jesus will tell you his will
Please listen and hear what the Lord has to say
Just open your mind and be happy all day
The sun will be shining so bright in the sky
As you go on your way and walk happily by
"faith"cfd

Last

I'm trying some things to stay above board
But I can't do it alone how I do need you Lord
Help me have patience help me to survive
All of the bees and all of there hives
I don't know that it's right I don't know that it's wrong
I just know I need help from you to get along
Tell me what's right or I'll fall flat on my face
Please tell me dear Jesus Please show me your grace
To know what I do is what's in your plan
And know when it's not by the touch of your hand
To understand darkness pain and despair
It's easier knowing that Jesus your there
To help me through and take me in
To keep me away from the worlds sin
So help me fix the things that are wrong
An keep me knowing with you I belong
And this won't go on forever and a day
That your my Master and your on your way
To help me get out of this terrible hole
And know that with Jesus I have a clean soul
It might not be easy it might not be fast
But when the King does it it's going to last
"faith"cfd

Promised

The birds are out the sun is bright
The day has taken away the night
The earth is warm the sky is blue
Jesus wants to talk to you
He wants to tell you he is here
And take away your awesome fear
To lift you up when you are down
And let you know he's always around
Just ask he'll hear you night or day
Believe he listens to what you say
There may not be immediate relief
For Gods sweet plans require belief
He's never said perfect we will be
Until the day his face we'll see
We must endure we must hold on
For someday our troubles will be gone
So we will do the very best we can
And hold onto the Masters hand
Someday it's promised we'll go home
And see God and Jesus on their thrown
"faith"cfd

Look and Find

Today as I look around this place
I pray to look on Jesus face
To see the splendor of his eyes
I know right then I'm going to cry
Like a baby crying in it's bed
He will touch me on the head
He will comfort me he'll bring me joy
As if to comfort a little boy
He will show me Heaven sweet
My God I just can't wait to meet
To love the Lord has been my quest
Please love God for he is the best
You'll never find a better friend
You can look until the very end
A better friend they'll never be
God's the very best friend for you and me

"faith"cfd

Not a Story

If not for Jesus my world would fall
But I have answered my Kings call
He tells me what I should do
And that's the things I try too
I try to do what he asks
And at times they are hard tasks
Tasks are hard the prize is great
Dear God I can hardly wait
To see your face shining bright
That will be a glorious sight
The King of Kings the Son of Man
The one that holds me in his hand
The one that comforts me when I am down
The King the Christ the one with the crown
A golden crown upon his head
Just like the one the Bible said
When I go home I'll see it all
Because he'll never let me fall
He'll help me stand against the grief
And the time will come for my relief
I'll go home to all his glory
Knowing it was not a story
                    "faith" cfd

Be Forgiven

Be quiet be still for he knows your heart
Stick with him and you'll never part
Hold your head up for a Christian you see
Will go to heaven with God and Jesus you'll be
Hold on to his hand and he'll make it all right
He'll come to you deep in the night
He'll come to you he'll knock at your door
For that's what Jesus has come here for
To open your eyes so you see the way
That Jesus wants you to go everyday
He'll talk to you so you will see
All the things he wants for you and me
He's opened the door for you to walk in
So lay down your sword be forgiven of your sin

"faith" cfd

Child be Patient

Go in peace my child be patient and wait
For Jesus is waiting at the great gate
I'll love you forever my precious one
The father mother daughter and son
I love all creation in his holy name
Because with God every bodies the same
Jesus loves us the same and we are holy blessed
And space has been saved in his holy nest
We'll see all the things compassionate and true
Cause we've done everything he's ask us to
                              "faith"cfd

Open my eyes

To be my Lord I have to be proved
My love for you cannot be moved
I must be true to thee
And let me see what you want from me
To call upon the Lord so great
And put me in a gospel state
Let me know that I am worthy
For sometimes it feels so very unnerving
Take me home dear Lord I pray
For ever with you I want to stay
Open my eyes and show me direction
For it may not be the same as my notion
Open my eyes so I can see
All the things you have for me
All things from God are always good
Just make me see how you think I should
                              "faith"cfd

Not Alone

Dear Jesus my precious understanding God
Some day in Heaven please let me trod
Please let me see your brilliant face
When I get up there in that place
The place of sweet undying care
That God I hope will bring me there
To be with you my precious King
So I can see love is everything
Your love your peace your undying joy
For every little girl and boy
I don't mean the kids so much
But all the adults you've come to touch
                    "faith"cfd

One Day

Heaven is a glorious place
To see the Lord Gods awesome face
To see the King Jesus the Son of Man
With them I will do all I that can
For the scripture says to us when we read
They'll see us through each and every need
There here beside us they'll hold our hand
They help us through they will help us to stand
We stand on everlasting Love
That comes straight from above
Rains down on us as we go through
The trails the devil draws us to
So heads stay up and smiles stay on
One day we'll be with God and his Son
                    "faith"cfd

Win

God the Master God the Father
God the mother sister and brother
God wants all the people to be one
That's why he sacrificed Jesus his Son
To care for us and make us see
Everything that we should be
Close knit and helpful to the good and the bad
But the way we do things just makes him sad
For this is not what he wanted to see
God wants help from you and from me
Help to bring the sinners in
Not just family and not just kin
But any body that you can bring in
And let Jesus wash away all there sin
God will smile when he sees what you've done
And Jesus will smile for each and every one
Every day talk about Jesus the King
For there may not be time to do anything
But any where that you might be
Is some one God wants us to see
To Heaven that's right bring every one
You can win over to Jesus The Son
God will help you he'll give you the words
To tell all the people to let loose the sword
Be patient says God the time will come soon
And the sinners will be left to look up at the moon
"faith"cfd

Love and Trust

God is love God is forever
He'll leave us no not ever not ever
He'll be there beside us with his open arms
Protecting us forever from the devils harms
Jesus knows all our fears
It may not seem that he is near
But just know that Gods love is always here
He'll never give up till he sees us there
For God and his Jesus do really care
They know you down to the very last hair
They hurt when we hurt they cry when we cry
They even feel sad when we barely get by
All they want is for us to succeed
They furnish us with all that we need
For God is so patient he's kind and he's true
But he may not do what you want him to
So you must trust in the Lord and know that he's right
And be glad you have what you have tonight
Some people don't have a nice bed to lay on
And babies everyday in poverty are born
So be faithful although little there may be
For some aren't as lucky as you and as me
We need to help people as Christ have us do
And bring a smile to a person or two
Be thankful be kind be helpful and true
Do everything that our Lord ask of you
Take heed for the Bible tells what you should do
Be faithful and cautious for the time will be soon too
                                "faith"cfd

Drums

Christ the Lord is coming soon
It may be the light of the moon
You must always be ready
You must always be steady
In the love of the Lord is where you must be
And the love of the Lord is what you must see
For Christ is the Master and he is our King
And for Jesus we must do anything
We must go for the prize
And see Christ through our eyes
So to Heaven we'll go when the day comes
And no fear will there be when we hear the drums
"faith"cfd

Fear

It's now the time to know the Lord
It's time dear friend give up your sword
For Christ could come most any day
And here you'll be if with sword you stay
Be smart take heed take God in your heart
He's the one who'll know your smart
With God you'll go to heaven you see
You'll go with the others you'll go with me
When the time comes and Jesus is near
Don't be scared don't be in fear
So just believe in Jesus as your King
Believe with God you can do anything
Believe that Christ loves you and loves me
Be patient and kind with Jesus You'll see
He loves us he does he'll do anything
Just believe in the Lord and that day you will sing
You'll see the bright light and with Jesus you'll smile
Because with Jesus you'll live for a long long while
"faith"cfd

A Prayer for the People
Dear Lord my Savior strong and true
Please bless these people who have come to you
To worship the Lord of all creation
Please bless this loving congregation
Relieve the hurt depression or pain
In your loving presence please let us remain
Give us the strength to cope each day
And guide us dear lord along our way
Please help us to spread around the land
The love that flows from your loving hand
Embed in our hearts the love for each other
And the desire to help our sister and brother
Forgive us the things we have failed to do
The times we don't do what you want us to
And the times we do what we know is wrong
Please guide us Lord as we struggle along
We praise you and thank you for Jesus your Son
And pray that we see you when life here is done
Your love is much more than we could ever repay
Thank you dear Lord for your presence today
                                        "faith"cfd

When He Comes

Oh people Oh people what will you do
When Jesus the Christ comes here for you
Will you be ready will you be right
For Jesus could come deep in the night
There's no telling when the Savior will come
Will all your work on earth here be done
Are there things left undone that you should do
Because Jesus the Christ will not wait for you
He'll come and he'll take only those that are ready
He'll take only the ones with him that are steady
To know the steadfast love of the Lord
He will not take the people who have lived by the sword
Take heed dear people that Christ will be here
And all those sinners will kneel down in fear
Then it's to late there is no time left now
Your stuck on this earth there's no need to bow
For people have told you that the time would come
And how many choose not to get here things done
Believers are sorry for those left behind
They tried and and the tried that Jesus you'd find

(cont.)

When He Comes (cont.)
We'll say hello Master we'll praise his sweet name
For Christ the Jesus is always the same
He has always loved us he's always been there
We even tried scripture to show how God does care
To make you into believers to bring you to the fold
But all that you have you continue to hold
You hold on to money land and power
That stuff won't help you in Jesus great hour
Take heed repent give your self to the Lord
You can't get into heaven when you carry a sword
You must carry your cross take up with the Lord
So take up your cross and lay down the sword
Go to your knees before it's to late
Pray to God to alter your fate
Pray Jesus forgive me before my times up
And lead me to heaven to drink from your cup
That's what we pray all over the place
That everyone gets to see Jesus face

"faith"cfd

I Pray

Lord I want to come home if I could
I think I've done all that I should
I've tried to be kind I've tried to be true
Lord I think I've done the things I should do
I've tried to treat people the way that you ask
I've tried to smile with every task
I've tried not to sin against your law
I've prayed to you when my sin I saw
I don't expect to get in with works that I've done
For I know salvation is loving Jesus the Son
To believe in Jesus is what it's about
To love him and praise him to stand up and shout
To spread his word wherever I go
Just one person I hope I helped Jesus to know
Not to say that one is enough
For spreading the word can be so tough
But if I helped save one I've done a great deed
I hope there are many I've tried to sow seed
I hope everybody here on this earth
Will come to know about Jesus birth
His preaching his teaching his great love
That comes from his heart and it comes from above
So I'll pray till the end till the time will come
I know many will be saved but there will be some
That never have known Jesus as he wanted them to
And I'll keep trying to do all I can do
I pray to you Jesus stay deep in my heart
I pray I'll stay steadfast and we'll never part
I love you Jesus and I'll keep trying
For sinners I don't want to see crying
Until you return to this place
And I see your beautiful face
                    "faith" cfd

Just Love Me
Dear God of amazing grace
Humble us when we see your face
God loving and kind you've been
Take me back to your house to spend
Eternity and life so sweet
To kneel down Jesus at your feet
Watch over me cleanse my mind
That all your glory I will find
Your love that's greater then them all
Jesus keep me from a fall
For Heavens where I want to be
Take me Lord and just love me
                    "faith"cfd

Favor
Here's the day it's morning now
I drop to my knees and again I'll bow
To ask the mornings love fulfill
For all the people that will
And hold my shoulder and steer me straight
So I will go through heavens gate
And at your precious feet I'll kneel
And hear your voice with that great zeal
Well done my child you've done me well
And of these works I won't ask you to tell
You've done your job you've done it right
And you find favor in my sight
                    "faith"cfd

Lost

Be happy people if you can see
A light deep in your heart will be
The light of God that shines so bright
That you can see it in the night
Night and day you'll feel the pull
To do the right thing for your heart is full
Full of love for the Almighty King
Knowing in God you can do anything
Sowing the seed to all that you meet
And laying your burdens at the Kings feet
Just keep your heart open let Jesus stay in
Don't give into the devil's wicked sin
Keep your heart open be still and just wait
For your time will come to enter the gate
The gate of Heaven I'm referring to
So keep steadfast in all that you do
Be patient for the time you know not of
But remember pray for you God does love
Pray for the people that don't know the Lord
And pray that everyone will lay down the sword
Pray for the lost yes pray for the others
The fathers mothers sisters and brothers
They haven't found Christ our Almighty God
For if there not saved in Heaven they won't trod
What an unhappy thought to just know sin
For when the time comes the ice will be thin
To thin to stand on they'll fall right through
For it will be to late and nothing they can do
And when the time comes the sinners will stay
Because they've chosen sin all the way
Now is the time to help sinners to see
For God wants in Heaven the sinners to be
                                    "faith"cfd

He's Close

Sit outside and feel the breeze
Let God set your mind at ease
For nature is a wonderful thing
All year long not just in the spring
It has a soft and lovely lull
Just close your eyes and hear Gods call
He wants you to be relaxed and free
God has a plan for you and me
A plan we may not understand
But know God holds you by the hand
He's close to you just stop and feel
He's here for you to help you deal
With all your problems great and small
The Almighty will help you through them all
He'll laugh with you he'll cry with you
He'll show you what you need to do
Be patient and pray and wait on the Lord
Take up your cross lay down your sword
For one day you'll be going home
To see your God upon his thrown
"faith" cfd

A Place

Daylight has come again
Another day to begin
Make this a day you can remember
Light that fire that's just an ember
Go to the Lord and confess your sin
And a new life you will begin
Take up your cross and follow God
And one day Heavens soil you'll trod
He just wants to help you through
All the things that you must do
He just wants to see your face
For in Heaven you will have a place
A place of love and joy and peace
A place where earthly troubles cease
                              "faith" cfd

Take the Hand

Take the Master by the hand
Let him lead you to the promise land
Open up your heart today
God won't have it any other way
He's here he's there he's everywhere
He wants only his love to share
For you are Gods blessed child
Be calm be meek try to be mild
For God so loved the world it seems
He gave his Son to fulfill his dreams
He'll lift you up when you are down
Remember child he's always around
He's wherever you may be
He's always here for you and me
Just let go and feel his love so awesome
If you do with God you will come
And be a part of his great family
For God the Father you will see
                              "faith" cfd

Gods Hand

People give up let go of your sin
Only with Jesus can you win
He's the only way to live your life
All things will pass including your strife
In Heaven you'll see Jesus the King
He wants only good he sees everything
He cries when his children go a stray
So lay down your sin go to Jesus today
The time will come and will you be ready
Have you been strong have you been steady
Have you loved the Lord like you should
All God wants is for us to be good
He wants us to love everybody in peace
So all turmoil and trials can finally cease
So we can go home to the promise land
Holding the best holding Gods hand
"faith"cfd

The Blood

The greatest thing that I've ever felt
Is when Jesus took my sin and with it he dealt
The peace I've known since he took me in
And washed me in his blood taking away all my sin
And when I backslide he's still there
Because he loves me and does really care
He drapes me in his love and all his kindness
And helps me take away all my blindness
So I can see what he is here for
And know that someday I'll go through the door
That door that door the pearly gates
For believers go to Heaven the Bible it states
Heaven oh Heaven a beautiful place
I'll go to Heaven and I'll see his face
The face of the Almighty the face of the King
The face of a friend who can do anything
"faith"cfd

Ultimate One
We all have sinned by the way we are living
But pray to the Lord and all will be forgiven
Take heed watch yourself for Jesus does see
All that we do yes you and yes me
He watches from his thrown above
And do not doubt him of his love
His love is lasting his love is sure
His love helps us to endure
Jesus is the ultimate love
He sits upon a thrown above
He loves us everyday and night
The King never lets us out of his sight
He only wants the best you see
That's why he loves you and me
He's here he wants only our love
So we can go to him like a dove
Fly to him when life is done
For Jesus is the ultimate one
"faith" cfd

Heartache

Oh Father please forgive me for I have sinned
Take away my heartache throw it to the wind
Take me and mold me just how I should be
And help me to love and help me to see
Take hold of my hand and lead me there
Where finally I won't have any care
Please help me if you only would
I love you but not as much as I should
Everlasting in your grace please let me see
All your love indwelling me
Teach me to pray everyday and every night
Teach me how to hold to you so tight
Let me do whatever you want me to
I'll try my very best the tasks I will do
Someday dear Jesus I want to come home
And see you and God on your great thrown
                    "faith"cfd

Repent of Your Sins

There is a such thing as the pearly gates
And behind them my God and my Jesus awaits
They await my homecoming for it is true
I'll go to Heaven if I do what they ask me to
I picture Heaven as a white fluffy cloud
And only believers will be allowed
For God won't let just anyone in
You have to repent of all your sin
Repent daily for we are human you see
We sin we do although we don't want it to be
We are human we don't pay attention at all
But thanks to the Master we're caught when we fall
So go on your days and do what is right
And you'll have a place in our Masters sight
                    "faith"cfd

Love Lifts
God lifted me out of the pit
And sinning I'm trying hard to quit
Love lifted me out of the hole
For Jesus wants to save my soul
Save my soul and set me free
And take me where I need to be
Beside me always he will stand
When ever I go through out the land
He'll always be there through good and bad
A better friend I've never had
He lifts me up when I am down
He makes a smile out of a frown
He comforts me he loves me so
This is a thing I really do know
With God the Father and Jesus the Son
Everything I can do I just know that I've won
There love lifts me up all of the day
And I know it's suppose to happen that way
"faith" cfd

It's Morning

Good morning Lord I hear the birds
I'm ready again to hear your words
I'll kneel and pray as I should
Because it makes me feel quite good
I linger in the quietness
Before my mind starts to stress
Stress over the things gone wrong
Instead I'll opt to sing a song
A song of old Amazing Grace
Helps me to closer see your face
And helps me be steadfast in your way
For this is a new beautiful day
A day of a new beginning
A day to be praising and singing
Another day to love you more
For that's what you ask me for

"faith" cfd

Dad Is The Best Ever
Down through the years I grown to see
All the love he has selflessly given to me
Dependent on him to help work things out

It's what my friend my Dad is about
Strong and forceful yet gentle and kind

The type of man that is so hard to find
Helping to calm me when no one else can
Ever so loving yet hard to understand

Because he's been such a dear friend to me
Ever in his debt I know I will be
Stronger my love for him continues to grow
That is so important and I want him to know

Eternally grateful for Dad Lord it's true
Very much do I love him God you know that I do
Every step that he takes please guard him for me
Right up to the day when heaven he'll see
"faith" cfd

Follow You

It's raining outside such weather we've had
First rain and then snow it's been pretty bad
But I know it all comes down from up above
That's a way you show your undying love
To replenish the earth which is so needed
Well dear Lord I think you really succeeded
For when the wind blows I can remember your death
For it's a way to send us your precious breath
To let us know you can do anything
With all you stand for such pleasure it brings
The pleasure of knowing that all of your love
Comes to us from the King up above
To know that the weather is just one thing
That I very soon will witness the spring
When flowers come out and the earth renews
And takes away the wintertime blues
To witness the beauty of the flowers and sun
Is when sinners turn there backs and run
Help me to help sinners to open a crack
So we can draw sinners that haven't come back
That the small seed we sow can grow in their heart
And we will know that we've done our part
Just sow the seed and pray it will grow
That's all we really need to know
I pray the sinners will obey the way
Oh how that would be a glorious day
To see all people follow you home
On the special day you come down from your thrown
                    "faith" cfd

Freely Fly

You wake up in the morning still half asleep
And look around to see out the window you now peek
To see if he sun will shine or if the rain will fall
It doesn't really matter for Jesus hears your call
Pray in the morning to start you day off right
And enjoy that God's been with you all through the night
He longs to hear your praying he listens and he hears
Every word your saying that might even bring some tears
God's happy when you talk to him It tends to bring a smile
So go to God each morning and wait with him awhile
He'll tell you what he wants from you today
When your done, your work he'll send you on your way
Pray for the Master to make your spirit strong
Every thing you try to do will never come out wrong
Someday he'll take you home, No more bad to see
And glory will over power you the beauty that will be
Heaven is so beautiful a sight for weary eyes
For when Jesus comes the white dove will freely fly

"faith"cfd

Confession

I've written a lot over the years
Some have even brought some tears
But one thing I do know for sure
There is a Godly open door
A greater presence we cannot see
But know he's there with you and me
He knows we listen he knows we care
He knows how much we try to share
So be trustful and open hear his word
For he could be watching as a bird
He could be watching in any form
To see how we weather our secret storm
He wants your secret to be open and true
No secrets from God this he wants from you
So confess all your sins and make it right
So you can sleep in peace tonight
Be cautious for deception can be your downfall
And even effect us one and all
So open your mind and see
You need to be where God wants you to be

"faith"cfd

Redeeming

God's love is not earned it comes to us so free
It depends on what you do with it that's up to you and me
We have the gift of choice God has made it just this way
He'll love us all but sinners need repentance bad today
For time may be running out we do not know just when
For Christ Jesus you must know he wants to let you in
He wants your heart and his love he sends it from up above
You just have to believe in him and except his glorious love
He'll keep you safe from all temptation you only do his will
He knows your heart with him better you will feel
God takes the trouble in your life and then you must endure
For God loves his children of this you can be sure
Take time to hear the Master take time to hear his voice
Once you find the love of God your heart will just rejoice
God will take your heart and you the good of believing
For all Christians find a reel since of Gods redeeming

"faith"cfd

Home

Home is where the heart surrounds
All the loving family sounds
The place where dinners cook away
The place where all the loved ones stay
The quiet humble place so safe and true
To do the things that families do
Children running here and there
While family in the home they share
Stories of the days gone by
Some that even make family cry
Home is where the heart abides
And home is always in Gods watchful eyes
For home is just and earthly place
For someday we will see Gods face
Until then we'll struggle on our way
Until home in eternity we will stay
"faith"cfd

Someday
You made it through another day
Don't forget the Lord remember to pray
So many of Gods children have grown apart
They no longer feel God in there heart
Pray for all people that they will see
How wonderful a Christian they could be
Praise God I have a shoulder to lean on
For someday we'll have Dear Jesus to adore
With praise and thanks giving for Christ the Lord
For when he comes back we can lay down our swords
Lay down the heavy armor of God
By then we will be walking on heaven sod
Glorious place with silver and gold
More riches that even the saints have told
Be patient and wait upon our God
So someday we will see that beautiful heavenly sod
So he'll bring us home one day I'll see
The beautiful face of God and Jesus will be
So hold on to that thought for Jesus comes soon

cont.

someday (cont)
And snatches us up like a helium balloon
God is good all the time
Listen he will help you make up your mind
He'll be there for ever mountain we have to climb
He's here among us all of the time
We may pray and when we sing to the Lord
He will be pleased to know we kept our word
Be good to your neighbors as they were your kin
To a sinful life and there will be sin
Just hold on tight to the King on high
Even if life seems to be passing you by
For someday God, Jesus and the Holy Ghost
Well come for those who have adored him the most
Hold on tight don't let your emotions kick in
For Jesus knows our trouble and our sin
But just ask sincerely he will take you in
And cleanse you and love you in spite of your sin
Jesus is the only great King he's the only way
That can take you up where we will stay
The King, the Power and the Holy Ghost
Are what we want to see the most
                    "faith"cfd